For B.M.

You fly so close to the sun…

Praise for *Kinda Christianity*

"The main story was so compelling the first time through I just couldn't put it down. The second time through, what I would call the hiddeness of the book just grabbed me. The third time something new and different. When you get it into your hands, I encourage you to read it many times. This is not a one-time read and it will be forever a part of who I am."
- BOBO BRAZIL, Professional Wrestler

"So if my scoring is correct, Ted is riding Kevin's theological credibility coattails, you're riding Ted's, and I'm a couple emergent trolls away from riding yours. I'm not sure what that sentence even means, but it sounds deep enough to try."
-MIKE WITTMER, Author, *Don't Stop Believing*

"Great stuff, guys. Seriously, great freakin' stuff."
-THE VENERABLE BEDE, 7th Century Monk

"We talkin' about orthopraxy? Orthopraxy?!"
- ALLEN IVERSON, NBA Star

"Riveting, with twists that defy your expectations while teaching powerful theological lessons without patronizing. I was crying by page 10. You cannot read it without your heart becoming involved."
- BRIAN URLACHER, Middle Linebacker, Chicago Bears

"Nein! Just...nein."
- KARL BARTH, Theologian

"Your work is a masterpiece! There are tears in my eyes and a lump in my throat."
- JIM PALMER, Baltimore Orioles

"Melissa, send these guys my standard blurb. (Hold the '*stand up and cheer*' stuff this time) -Jim"
-J.I. PACKER, Author and Endorsement-Smith

"Haw! Haw! Haw!"
- JACK CHICK, Renowned Author and Conspiracy Theorist

"I read and wept and slept and read again. I am full of words, inexpressible thoughts, shades and hues of hope and light and joy."
- FLOZELL ADAMS, Offensive Tackle, Dallas Cowboys

"Do you ever stand by the ocean, just close your eyes and breath deeply, filling your lungs with purity? That's what *Kinda Christianity* is like. I've filled my lungs with clean, fresh air, after choking on the stifling smog of religiosity. At times I had tears in my eyes, and others I was laughing out loud."
- RON KARKOVICE, Catcher, Chicago White Sox

"In every way, a dispatch from the front, it is also a love letter of sorts – a love letter from affectionate, seasoned writers to those who would dare to believe, worship, and serve not only now, but also beyond now, into the roiling, churning decades ahead."
- CORY HARTMAN, Age 12

"Ted and Zach are two distinct kinds of visionaries, sort of like fire and ice. I see myself as somewhere in the middle...like lukewarm water."
- DEREK SMALLS

"Before I met Ted and Zach, my life was, cosmically, a shambles. I was using bits and pieces of whatever Eastern Philosophy was drifting through my transom."
- DAVID ST. HUBBINS, Lead Singer, Spinal Tap

"By the quality of your ironic t-shirts, all men will know you."

- The Voice, John 13:35

KINDA CHRISTIANITY

A Generous, Fair, Organic, Free-Range Guide to Authentic Realness

TED KLUCK
ZACH BARTELS

"IT'S NOT TRUE THAT THE REASON NO ONE LIKES YOU IS BECAUSE THEY'RE JEALOUS. THEY DON'T LIKE YOU BECAUSE YOU'RE KIND OF A JERK."

I RECENTLY RECEIVED THAT AS A TWEET FROM A FRIEND OF MINE. IT'S A GREAT QUOTE, AND OF COURSE IT DOESN'T APPLY TO YOU PERSONALLY AT ALL -- IT APPLIES TO EVERYONE ELSE EXCEPT YOU.

I POINT THAT OUT BECAUSE TED AND ZACH WROTE A LITTLE HANDBOOK HERE WHICH, EVEN IF IT DOESN'T GO *THE SHACK* FOR THEM, IS GOING TO GET THE CRITICISM, "THEY'RE JUST A BUNCH OF JERKS, DUDE." TED WILL BE CALLED A HATER OR MAYBE SOME KIND OF MISOGYNIST HOMOPHOBE JOCK, AND ZACH WILL BE NAMED AS INFAMOUS IN SPITE OF HIS UBIQUITOUS USE OF HEBREW TO SPELL HIS FIRST NAME. (POSER)

BUT HERE'S THE THING: ARE *THEY* THE HATERS? IT SEEMS TO ME THAT THEY ARE NOT THE HATERS -- THEY ARE SIMPLY THE ONES WHO ARE *NOT JEALOUS*. THEY ARE NOT THE ONES CALLING EACH OTHER JOHN BUNYAN AND MARTIN LUTHER, NAMING THEIR MOVEMENT A "NEW REFORMATION" IN THE MIDST OF ALSO LOWERING MORAL STANDARDS, ELIMINATING THE THINGS WHICH ARE DISTINCTIVE ABOUT THE CHRISTIAN FAITH, AND DRESSING IN A SHABBY WAY RATHER THAN A WAY WHICH SAYS, "I AM IN THE IMAGE OF MY CREATOR, SO I WANT TO KEEP THE PLACE LOOKING NICE."

THAT IS, OF COURSE, NOT TO SAY THAT THE OBJECTS OF THE BRIGHT LIGHTS AND SHINY SHARP OBJECTS IN THIS BOOK ARE THE ONLY ONES WHO FLUB WHAT IT MEANS TO BE A CHRISTIAN. IT IS TO SAY, THOUGH, THAT THESE PEOPLE HAVE MADE AN ART OF IT. UNDER

THE GUISE OF DOING SOMETHING INDISPENSIBLE WITH A 2000-YEAR TRADITION OF PHILOSOPHICAL, POLITICAL, ECONOMIC, SOCIAL AND SPIRITUAL WINS THEY HAVE SIMPLY DONE WHAT GEORGE COSTANZA WOULD DO -- THEY HAVE DONE THE OPPOSITE.

WHAT TO DO IF THERE ARE GLARING MORAL ISSUES IN OUR DAY -- SPEAK IN A PROPHETIC VOICE ECHOING ISAIAH AND ELIJAH AND MOSES? OH HECK NO -- DO THE OPPOSITE: EMBRACE THE MORAL FAILINGS OF OUR DAY AND SAY THAT THIS IS WHO WE ARE. DON'T HATE ME BECAUSE I'M FABULOUS AND FAMOUS LIKE PEREZ HILTON OR SPENCER AND HEIDI.

WHAT TO DO WHEN WORSHIP IS ITSELF SOMETHING EVERYONE FINDS SOMEWHAT UNCONSCIONABLE AND UNFIT FOR OUR DAYTIMERS -- DRESS UP OUR TIME TOGETHER AND INFORM IT SO THAT WE CANNOT FORGET THAT WE'RE TALKING ABOUT THE CREATOR OF ALL THINGS, THINKING ABOUT HOW PAUL SPOKE TO THE FOLKS AT CORINTH OR MAYBE HOW THE WRITER OF HEBREWS PUTS TOGETHER A VISION OF OUR SAVIOR AND OUR FAITH? OH PLEASE -- DO THE OPPOSITE: PAINT THE PLACE BLACK, LIGHT A FEW CANDLES, AND SIT ON RATTY SOFAS AND TALK ABOUT *OURSELVES* AND THE STORY WE FIND OURSELVES IN. DON'T ASK MORE OF ME, BUT LESS.

AND WHILE WE'RE TALKING ABOUT US, HOW DO WE KNOW WHO "WE" ARE -- HOW DO WE KNOW WHAT THE CHURCH ITSELF IS, HERE AND NOW? DO WE RAISE UP LEADERS WHO ARE KIND AND DISCERNING MEN WHO ARE LEANING ON SCRIPTURE AND ON THE PROMISE OF CHRIST, WHO ARE USING BAPTISM AS A GATE TO BRING DISCIPLES TO CHRIST AND WHO ARE ADMONISHING THE PEOPLE OF GOD TO BELIEVE IN CHRIST AND LIVE AS IF HIS RESURRECTION IS TRUE THE WAY YOUR DVR SCHEDULE IS TRUE AND YOUR PAYCHECK IS TRUE? C'MON NOW: DO THE OPPOSITE! WE SHOULD BE

LOOKING UP TO GUYS WHO CAN'T BE BOTHERED TO JOIN WITH OTHER BELIEVERS FOR WORSHIP, WHO WON'T TELL PEOPLE ABOUT THE LIFE *AFTER* LIFE AFTER DEATH WHEN INTERVIEWED BY THE NATIONAL PRESS, WHO MUST HAVE A "NEW KIND OF CHRISTIANITY" RATHER THAN THE ONE THE REST OF US HAVE INHERITED, AND WHO SHAME PEOPLE WITH PASSIVE-AGGRESSIVE ZINGERS, THEN STOP TALKING WHEN ASKED WHAT THEY SPECIFICALLY MEAN BY THAT. AND AS FOR BAPTISM AND A SOLID HOPE IN THE RETURN OF CHRIST, WHO CARES? WHAT'S THAT GOT TO DO WITH MY FAVORITE TREAT AT STARBUCKS?

THERE'S NOTHING TO BE JEALOUS OF THERE, TO GET BACK TO MY POINT. THERE'S NOTHING TO BE JEALOUS OF IN A MOVEMENT THAT IS EXACTLY LIKE WHAT YOU FIND IN SPENCER'S AT THE MALL OR MAYBE WHAT'S IN THE USED RECORD JOINT ACROSS THE STREET -- PEOPLE WHO MIGHT IN SOME SENSE LIKE THE SMELL OF WHAT THEY ARE SELLING, BUT THEY ONLY LIKE YOU IF YOU ARE BUYING.

TED AND ZACH AREN'T BUYING IT, AND NEITHER AM I. HOWEVER, I DO HAVE A REALLY-COOL ON-LINE T-SHIRT SHOP WHERE YOU CAN BUY T-SHIRTS THAT SAY "SPURGEON IS MY HOMEBOY" OR "ORTHODOX GANGSTA", AND I ENCOURAGE YOU TO INDULGE YOURSELF SINCE TED AND ZACH CUT ME OUT OF THE COMMISSIONS FOR THIS BOOK. KIDS THESE DAYS ...

GRACE AND PEACE TO YOU,

FRANK TURK
HTTP://TEAMPYRO.BLOGSPOT.COM
HTTP://T-SHIRTS.ITURK.COM
TWITTER: FRANK_TURK
HATEMAIL: JONESTONY@GMAIL.COM   O1 APRIL 2010

AUTHORS' NOTE

We know that the late emergent church movement™ is pretty much dead. But if emergent taught us anything, it's that nostalgia sells. Hence this book, which is a guide to emerging, but is also a nostalgic look at a movement that shaped at least six years worth of evangelical history. Let's remember it together. This is a humble, generous, incarnational, missional, community-based, grassroots guide to becoming emergent. So roll up the sleeves of your intentionally distressed Dickies™ work shirt, made entirely out of recycled cardboard, and enjoy!

A few words about the intention of the book: This book isn't meant to spur dialogue. This book isn't meant to really encourage anyone. This book is meant to make people laugh, and that's it. Nothing more, nothing less. If you read Turk's foreword and thought to yourself, "Hmmm, I may be in the market for a new kind of Christianity; I'm just not sure," then put this book down, go to Barnes and Noble, and get a copy of *Why We're Not Emergent* (it's by a famous pastor and some sports guy). But if you've made up your mind—either way—we invite you to read on.

That being said, you may not find this book funny. That's okay. But promise us one thing: You won't go onto your very own special blogspace and write a long treatise on why this book is mean-spirited and wrong. This is satire. It's not meant to be taken seriously (unless you like it, and want to take it seriously—in that case, blog away!) And know that a similar book could easily be written about smug, young reformed types...and in fact that book *is* being written, by us!

Also: No part of this book was made from recycled material. And no portion of the proceeds will go to benefit anything, except the authors and their families. (We're not even giving Turk a cut.)

So you're ready to take the plunge. Ready to translate your quest into action!

Without defining yourself, and certainly without boxing yourself into one particular rigid way of doing theology or church, you're ready to become emergent. You have a username and clever screen name picked out at Emergent Village™, and maybe you've even begun having church in an empty warehouse in the industrial sector of your city.

If so, good for you! But those are just the first, baby steps in your journey (your dance, if you will) into Kinda Christianity. This book will help you along the rest of your uniquely creative path to super-terrific self-discovery.

In short, you need this book like Bono needs wraparound sunglasses. You need this book like you need a *Coexist* bumper sticker on your used Volvo. Read it. Drink it in like a thick, frothy glass of Guinness, or sip it like a tall, skinny, half-caf, no-foam, soy, caramel macchiato. Converse with it like you would, theoretically, converse with a real, live person. Live it, breathe it, and embody it.

Think of this book as a woman—pregnant with new possibilities, and ready to birth you into a new life of romance, adventure, and passion! Let it inform your decision-making on fashion, driving, eating, drinking, protesting, reading, writing and living as an emergent Christian! But most of all, DANCE WITH US!

1. FASHION

Thomas Aquinas began his magnum opus with the existence of a "first cause, Himself uncaused." But that's so propositional and so divisive! I mean, Aquinas did the best he could in his institutional, bounded-set world, but he wasn't nearly as deep as we are (he didn't even live in a co-op). Besides, Kinda Christianity is far more concerned with orthopraxy than orthodoxy. Deeds not creeds, man! So, having given ourselves permission to start over from scratch, we begin our prolegomena, instead, with a far more important and fundamental discussion—that of fashion and style. Let's jump right in.

Your most important fashion accessory, of course, is your pair of eyeglasses. If you're reading this and thinking, "But Ted and Zach, I don't need glasses," you're wrong on two levels. One, you're just flat-out over-thinking all of this. Two, it's impossible to look pensive, artsy, thoughtful, intellectual, interesting, and unique without the right set of glasses. For examples, do a quick Google Images search for Lisa Loeb or Rob Bell. These are the frames you're looking for.

Your second most important fashion accessory may be your scarf. Perhaps you're saying to yourself, "But Zach and Ted, I don't live in a cold weather climate." Again, you're over-thinking it. Free your mind, as they say, and the rest will follow. What we're trying to say, is that you need a scarf. Scarves can be worn over t-shirts and over sweaters, in such a way as to suggest, "Hey, I'm not just an average guy in a t-shirt, I'm a guy in a t-shirt and a scarf."

Speaking of t-shirts, this is an important sub-category. I can't overstate how important your t-shirt collection is. The very future of your ministry depends on it. In fact, stop reading right now and take a hundred bucks and go to Urban Outfitters (pauses, while readers go to Urban Outfitters). If we're not mistaken, Brian McLaren's Red-Letter, free-form translation of the Bible, includes an important passage that reads, "They'll know you by the quality of your ironic t-shirts."

(A note on style: These shirts need to be a size or two too small, be "ringers," and have a one-color graphic—the more obscurely confusing, the better. 1970s television shows work great.)

Here's a working list, minimum, of the t-shirts you need in your collection:

- **Che Guevara.** Even though you have no idea who this guy was or what he did, it's important that you have this t-shirt because it says something about rebellion, hope, love, peace, joy, prosperity, poverty, and fame.

- **Bob Marley.** Even though you probably think reggae music sucks (because it does), Bob Marley is an icon and it's important that you associate yourself with him, even if you're a slightly overweight, white former youth pastor from Fort Wayne.

- **Sports Teams**. It's important that people know you like these shirts ironically, because you obviously never played sports—being that they're modern, militaristic, misogynistic, and violent. Still, it's hard to beat the old Chicago White Sox logo. Anything from Canada is great too.

- **Bands**. Band shirts are a tricky animal. They need to be obscure enough so as to suggest that you're an appreciator of all things small, under-funded, and unpopular. Or they need to be shirts of bands that have since disbanded (Pedro the Lion works great here).

- **Indigo Girls**. They're lesbians.

EMERGENT QUIZ:

Who is this man? (See Fig. A)

A. The Keynote Speaker at last year's Youth Specialties convention.

B. The author of *An Emergent Manifesto of Hope*.

C. A bloodthirsty murderer whose motto was, "If in doubt, kill him."

D. Co-Star of the movie *Twilight: New Moon*

Fig. A

2. PERSONAL GROOMING

It's important that you don't shave, because shaving is for lame corporate people who do things like get regular paychecks and go to work in offices. Shaving says, "I don't care about the poor, the city, the environment, minorities, Darfur, or freeing Tibet one bumper sticker at a time."

As far as hair is concerned, here are some options:

- **Faux Hawks** (perhaps a little outdated)

- **Pompadours** (only if you're Dan Kimball)

- **Completely Bald** (shaven—but purposeful, not to hide the fact that you're old)

- **Anything Spiky or Intentionally Disheveled** (some nice wax, putty, gel, or mousse works well here)

- **White Guy Dreads** (this is the i-Ching of emergent hair—if you're a white guy who's committed enough to The Movement to dread out his hair, our ironic trucker caps are off to you.)

Emergent Makover: Before

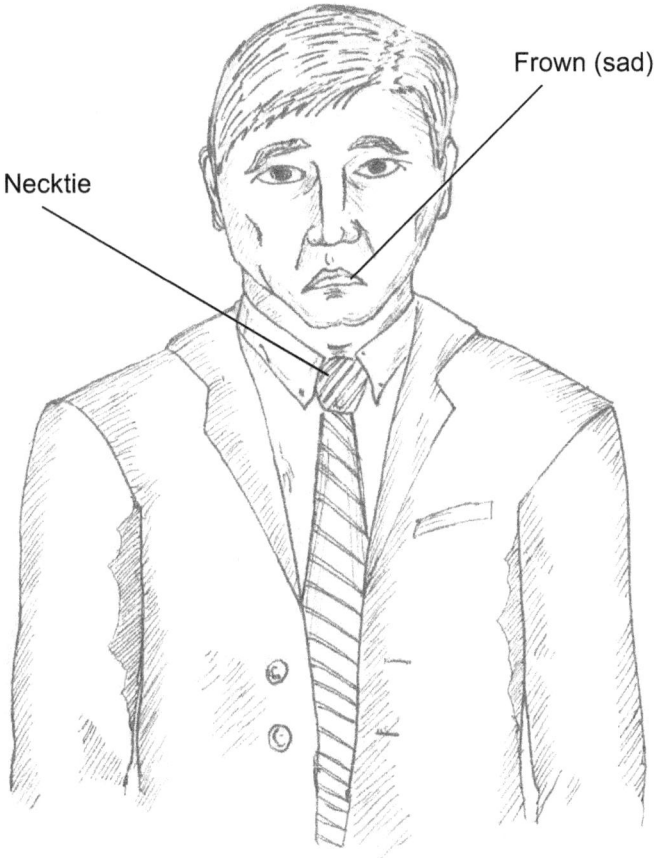

Would you trust this man to explain at length the spiritual significance of the latest Philip Seymour Hoffman movie? Me neither.

Note:
You may be thinking, "Ted and Zach, you seem to be speaking primarily to men. What about women's fashion and personal grooming?" That is a good question, so please keep it to yourself. To be perfectly frank, while "inclusiveness" is one of our favorite words, 95% of recognizable emergent figures are white, college-educated hipster males between the ages of 19 and 45.

This should in no way quell your passion for inclusiveness. Remember, people of all ages, races, creeds, coolness levels, and walks of life are free to join you at the spiritual gathering in the Starbucks across from campus. Or at the after-gathering hookah mellow.

Fig. C

Emergent Makover: After

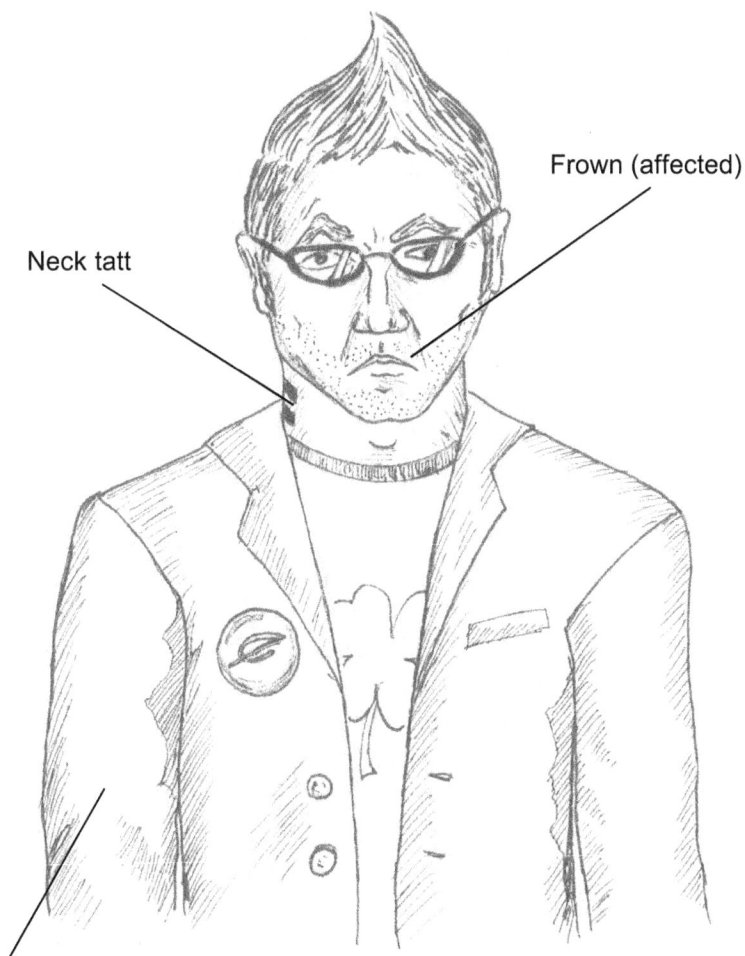

Neck tatt

Frown (affected)

Note the use of the same jacket. This is an important execution of the four R's—reduce, reuse, recycle, redeem culture.

9

3. WORKSPACE

This one is easy. If you're emergent, your workspace is nowhere, because the word "workspace" carries negative, corporate connotations. It carries gray, cubicle, break room, water-cooler type connotations, and those aren't cultures that you're interested in engaging. Let us tell you which culture you're called to engage: the one that meets at Starbucks.

Here's the thing. You need to get there early and get that one table in the corner where everyone who walks into the shop can see you, your Mac, and the very intentionally cool books that you're reading (anything by Dave Eggers, David Sedaris, Deepak Chopra, Kant, Derrida, Noam Chomsky, anyone philosophical or not more than one of the following: dead, white, male.)

It's important to hold/arrange these books in such a way that prompts people to ask, "Hey, what's that terribly interesting-slash-intellectually stimulating-slash-obscure book you're reading?" You cannot read any of the following:

- The Bible (unless it's a green-letter edition printed on soy-based recycled paper)
- CS Lewis
- Jonathan Edwards
- Anything by Ted Kluck, Kevin DeYoung, Mike Wittmer, or D.A. Carson.

Fig. D

If no one shows an interest in your 'work,' try relocating to
another train car, coffee shop, or fair-trade kiosk

Some Alternate Worksites Include:

- The steps of a museum or some other public building, if it's nice out. Of course you won't get any work done but it's important to be seen there.

- The library of the university you attended for nine years, receiving your dual degrees in Postmodern Feminist Thought and Urban Children's Literature.

- Any public transit. Here's the thing—you can sit on the subway all day, providing an endless array of people ample opportunity to ask you what you're working on.

- Really, wherever you and your backpack are gathered, there is a workspace.

4. VEHICLE

The first and foremost rule of thumb when choosing an emergent car is that it can't, under any circumstances, be domestic. Can you imagine Brian McLaren tooling around in a Chevy Malibu or a Ford F-150 Supercab? Me neither. Actually I can't imagine McLaren driving anything...I think he just floats around from treetop to treetop, like the characters in the PBS Kids environmentally-conscious program "Big, Big World."

Used Volvo wagons work well here, as do Subaru Outbacks, and any sort of Volkswagon van. Extra points for buying a car that runs on partially hydrogenated vegetable oil or your hatred for Dick Cheney.

Something to consider when buying your used car: the value of the bumper stickers. Look for stuff like "Coexist," the anachronistic "Impeach Bush," or a music festival that you wish you had attended. Where these bumper stickers exist, a good emergent car usually follows.

Better yet: A fixed-gear bicycle!

Fig. E

EMERGENT QUIZ:

Can you find the ten red flags indicating that this car is not a good emergent vehicle?

5. NAMES OF THINGS

Your church, of course, can't be called a church. You'll need to devise a name that incorporates your core values (rebellion, the environment, the city, being different, etc.).

To help in this endeavor we've created a handy *Emergent Church Name Generator* ™.

Instructions: Simply place a word from Group A in front of a word from Group B and you have the name of your church. It's that easy!

Group A:	Group B:
Black	Wind
Ecclesia	Fire
River	Sweat
Tribe	Tears
The	Soil
Solomon's	Rain
Blood	Street
Earth	Alley
Journey	Bono
	Betty

Examples:

- Black Betty
- Ecclesia Street
- Black Earth
- Earth, Wind and Fire
- Blood, Sweat, and Tears
- I've Seen Fire and I've Seen Rain…

Fig. F

Choosing the right evocative font is just as important as choosing the right name:

Tribe Alley

RIVER RAIN

Solomon's Tears

Avoid Papyrus Font entirely, as it is the sole property of the Institutional Church.

---

6. ATMOSPHERE

Apartment

When doing inner-city ministry (which is a pre-requisite for being emergent) it is important to get the right kind of city flat which is in a crummy enough neighborhood to be called "inner-city" but nice enough to be within walking distance of a Starbucks and afford the tenant a view of a capitol building or some other such "urban" landmark.

If you're really committed to The Cause, you may live in an apartment that has no furniture as a statement against the unethical treatment of furniture company employees. Or you may actually choose to live under a bridge, a la Shane Claiborne.

Worship Space

It's important that your church not look anything like a church, and in fact should not even be called a church (see also: names of things). It should look more like an abandoned meat-packing plant, complete with lots of exposed brick and ductwork. Big steel doors are nice. You'll also need a corner for the fully-functioning latte bar, one for the free-form liturgical finger-paint station, and lots of electrical outlets for the DJ stand, turntables, etc. And you'll need a large projection unit and screen for showing the Johnny Cash videos.

Fig. G

Where you live...

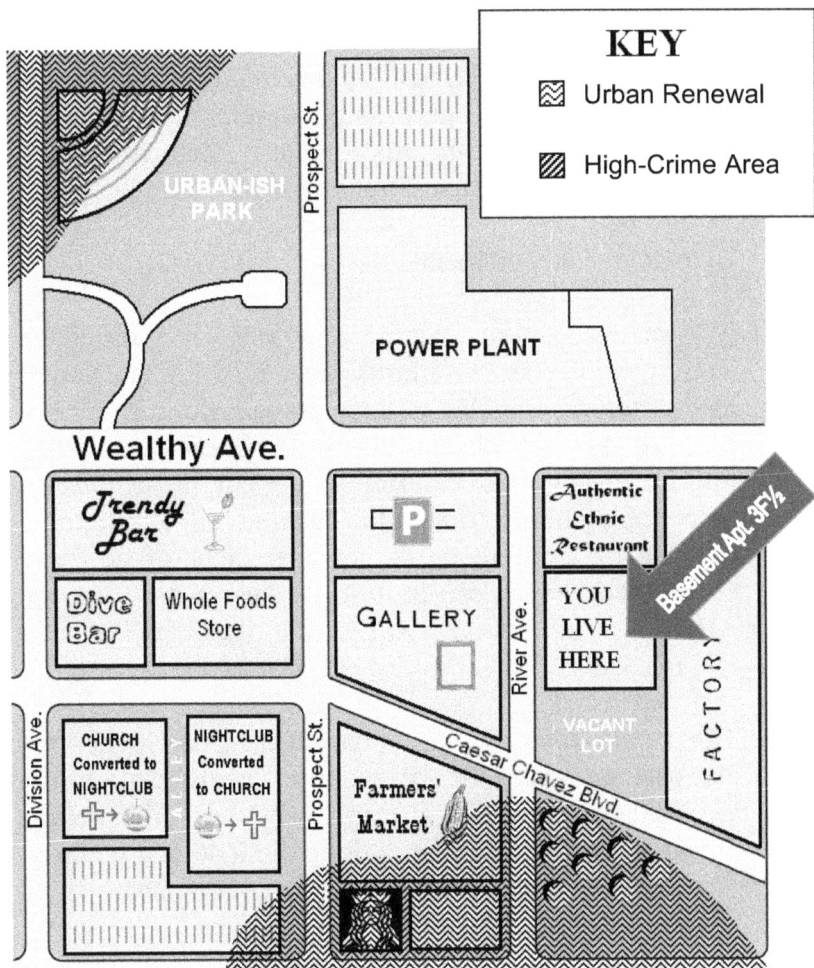

KEY
- ⬚ Urban Renewal
- ⬚ High-Crime Area

URBAN-ISH PARK

Prospect St.

POWER PLANT

Wealthy Ave.

Trendy Bar

Dive Bar

Whole Foods Store

P

GALLERY

River Ave.

Authentic Ethnic Restaurant

YOU LIVE HERE

Basement Apt. 3F½

VACANT LOT

FACTORY

Division Ave.

CHURCH Converted to NIGHTCLUB ✝→🪩

NIGHTCLUB Converted to CHURCH 🪩→✝

Prospect St.

Farmers' Market

Caesar Chavez Blvd.

19

7. YOUR INTERNET SPACE

In order to truly embrace Kinda Christianity, one must employ a very intentionally-cultivated online persona. The first, and most important, part of this persona is your blog. It's important to blog so that people can be exposed to your innermost feelings on a regular basis and then have the opportunity to remind you how open-minded, kind-hearted, and fabulous you are (enable the comments, but turn moderation on).

Here are the key elements:

A Name: Naming an emergent blog is a lot like naming a church, as it turns out. You'll glean your name from any number of sources—a lyric from a U2 song (good), an obscure word in Greek that you learned during the semester you spent in seminary before being burned out on the "institution" of religion (better), or a reference to some element of coffee, caffeinated beverages, or obscure dark beers (best). Any of these options will create the vibe you're looking for.

The Look: Even though you're against being showy and ostentatious in theory (see also: having church in an abandoned meat-packing plant), you'll spend upwards of 40 man-hours crafting the look and feel of your blog, so that your blog can communicate the uniquely creative vibe that you're going for. Part

Fig. H

A sample posture: thoughtful, somewhat vexed by the overwhelming challenge before you, but still approachable. You want your body language to communicate: "Yes, I'm working hard on my blog, but I'd gladly take a break to tell you about my blog."

of being emergent is being uniquely creative. Remember that none of the other 30-something, white, former youth pastors who rock retro tees and soul patches are anything like you. You're amazing. As such upwards of two-thirds of your church's budget should be pumped right into web development. All twelve of your members will benefit from an amazing online presence!

So what are the specific elements of "The Look?"

I. **Pictures of you** surrounded by poor, foreign children. "What does this have to do with me?" you might ask. The answer is "everything." Your readers need to know that you're not some callow, pasty, affluent white guy living in an overpriced flat with a view of the capitol building, drinking overpriced coffee in a gentrified part of the city. They need to know that you're the kind of guy who gets his picture taken with impoverished children (preferably on an actual trip to a Third World country, like Ecuador or Uganda). I can't overstate this. If you're not the kind of guy who is called to get his picture taken with these kinds of children, you need to re-evaluate your call to Kinda Christianity.

II. **Causes**. This goes hand in hand with number one. In order to be emergent you have to champion the right causes. Here are a few to choose from: organic free-range chickens, thinking globally and buying locally, the fact that if you're not angry you're not paying attention, recycling, love and how it wins, fair-trade coffee. The point is that you have to be fired up about something other than the Gospel, because being fired-up about the Gospel is the territory of closed minded judgmental young reformed people who live in Grand Rapids. And your readers need to know what you're fired up about.

III. Animation and Fonts. This is absolutely critical. Your website needs to look like an emo band's myspace page, and not, under any circumstances, a church. There needs to be some animation, and at least three links to short films made by your members. If your members aren't the kinds of people who make short films, maybe they need to re-evaluate their own call.

8. PEOPLE YOU LIKE

- Bono
- Bob Dylan
- John Dominic Crossan
- Eminem

- Jim Wallis
- Rob Bell
- Brian McLaren
- The Dalai Lama

Fig. I

- Shane Claiborne
- Moby
- Phyllis Tickle
- Bill Walton
- Alec Baldwin

- Phish
- Sufjan Stevens
- The guy from Pedro the Lion
- Anyone Else Who Makes You Feel Bad About Being White and Affluent

9. PEOPLE YOU DON'T LIKE

- D.A. Carson
- John Piper
- People Who Don't Feel Bad About Being White and Affluent
- Kevin DeYoung
- Ted Kluck
- Mike Ditka
- Ronald Reagan
- George Bush
- Mike Wittmer
- John Calvin
- Stephen Baldwin
- Mark Driscoll
- R.C. Sproul

Fig. J

10. DEALING WITH CRITICS
(PACIFISM)

You're too good, noble, pacifistic, and virtuous to really care what critics think. Also, you're too busy feeding the poor, raising money for your 5K run to combat Rainforest Gentrification, and managing the comments on your blog. However, you really DO care what the critics think!! Arrggh. Those (expletive) critics!! They don't get you. They're misrepresenting you. And they're taking you completely out of context.

Here's what you do: Spend a ton of time on the blogosphere, finding anyone whose ever written anything that could be construed as negative about you, postmodernism, your friends, or Kinda Christianity. Next, hijack that person's blogs and message boards with long, impassioned, poorly punctuated screeds on all the reasons why they're wrong and you're right. You absolutely can't, under any circumstances, let them get away with this! And no spell check. You don't have time for it, and it's not "authentic." If people don't love you regardless of your tense shifts and comma splices, there's no place in the kingdom for them.

Besides, who kneeds (sic) these people with their stupid, arkayic (sic) boundary-minded, bounded-set thinking?

Fig. K

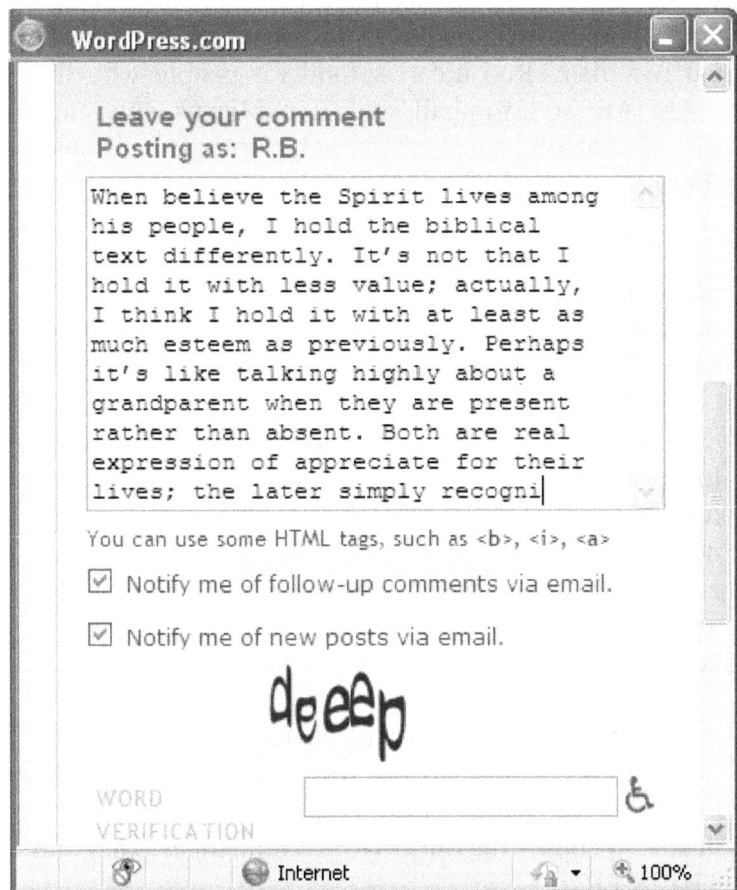

WordPress.com

Leave your comment
Posting as: R.B.

When believe the Spirit lives among his people, I hold the biblical text differently. It's not that I hold it with less value; actually, I think I hold it with at least as much esteem as previously. Perhaps it's like talking highly about a grandparent when they are present rather than absent. Both are real expression of appreciate for their lives; the later simply recogni

You can use some HTML tags, such as <b>, <i>, <a>

☑ Notify me of follow-up comments via email.

☑ Notify me of new posts via email.

deeep

WORD
VERIFICATION

Internet   100%

11. DIET

In order to retain a lithe, willowy (read: hungry) figure, you'll need to very intentionally plan your diet. It's important that you never, under any circumstances, eat red meat. Red meat is food for people who like NASCAR and football and Republicans and guns. This is not for you. Fish is okay, provided it's sushi (but nothing else). No fowl.

Ideally, you would subsist entirely upon raw, green leafy vegetables and legumes. The raw foods market in town (next to the used record store, adjacent to the Planned Parenthood clinic) is your friend.

One important exception to this rule: if you are lucky enough to find yourself in an authentic ethnic restaurant, owned and patronized by authentic ethnic people, then you are allowed to eat meat if a suitably ethnic vegetarian dish is not available. Your strident multi-culturalism can always pull rank on your conscience and palate.

Most importantly, it's critical that people every-where KNOW your dietary restrictions! Embrace this as part of the unique culture that is YOU! And if this makes people uncomfortable, remember that it's THEIR PROBLEM.

Fig. L

Remember, you owe it to meat-eating slobs to make plain your spiritual objections to their unsustainable, unhealthy, un-emergent lifestyle.

12. PLACES TO BE SEEN
(AND NOT SEEN)

Seen:

- Starbucks: This is your cathedral. This is your Holy Land. It goes without saying that this is where your people are.

- Trader Joes (or any other upscale Farmer's Market): This is where you spend upwards of two-thirds of your work time picking out exactly the right wine for communion.

- The Outdoors.

- Bars (both divey and upscale): It's important that people know that you're not only okay with drinking, but you like it! Just make sure you budget for all of the Guinness you're about to consume!

- Jazz Festivals. Duh.

- Community Theatres.

- Protest Marches.

- South America.

- The Apple Store: If you're not buying your technology here, you're not emergent. It's as simple as that.

- Kevin DeYoung's blog, ripping Kevin DeYoung.

- Tattoo parlors: Tattoos are "authentic," and make you unique. Nobody else has these!

- Urban Outfitters. That "Ms. Pac Man" t-shirt you've been pining away for isn't going to buy itself!

- Conferences that aren't conferences and don't feel like conferences. Ideally, your conference will be called a "gathering", be unscheduled, be completely un-planned, and take place in a bombed out building in the inner city where there will be music, coffee, and lots of sharing.

Not Seen:

- Church.

- Any large sports arena.

- Any mainstream movies (more on emergent cinema later).

- www.emergentvillage.com. Because it's dead.

- Chain Grocery Stores and Restaurants. These are the fruit of the devil (the devil being large corporate entities). Exceptions being Starbucks and Trader Joes.

Fig. M

34

13. THINGS YOU DO
(HOBBIES)

- Pledge your financial support to things like NPR, PBS, Greenpeace, and the World Wildlife Federation (but only to get the hand-woven shoulder bag made of recycled canvas and automobile tires).

- Write bad poetry.

- Question things.

- Tell people what you heard when you were listening to NPR this morning...

- Go to poetry slams to listen to other peoples' bad poetry.

- Bicycle. But never with the intention of racing or competing in any way.

- Make horrible short films meant to "inspire dialogue and build community."

- Try to learn to play the guitar. Fail.

- Play sports with no winner and no loser, like hacky sack. (Well, no winner, anyway...)

- Champion every cause, everywhere. If you're not angry, you're not paying attention!

I'M PRO-CAUSE & I VOTE!!

Fig. N

APPENDIX A – THEOLOGY

This section is admittedly something of an afterthought, because you're not into theology. Your "theology" is much more about what you're doing than about what God has done. And for a brief rundown of the things you're passionate about, one only needs to look here: www.moveon.org.

Still, at some point you may be expected to explain your theology. Here's a good place to start:

"I hurt myself today, to see if I still feel."
"I still haven't found what I'm looking for."
"Everybody hurts, sometimes."

And if all else fails, play the song "Bring Me To Life" by Evanescence, and do an interpretive dance to it. That should tell them all they need to know. If THAT fails...reference this *Guide to Kinda Christian theology:*

The 3 Rules of Kinda Christian Theology

1. Always strive to sound deep. Don't actually talk about what you believe directly (after all, "believe" is a Greco-Roman, bounded-set category). Instead, wax poetic about "something trying to be born from the womb of a better future" or about "harmonizing, dancing, sacred eco-systems." This makes you sound ridiculous to most people, but very deep to a few. And

it's those few who buy your books or read your blog, so they're the ones who matter.

2. Be unspeakably smug, and call it "humble."

3. Remember, the only absolute truth in Kinda Christianity is the goodness of "The Conversation" (may it be forever praised). If you are ever tempted to make a definitive statement not about the goodness of The Conversation, just ask a question instead.

Tactics

Pretend you know Hebrew and Greek. You'll probably get them wrong at every turn, but luckily, the people who will notice are not the people you're talking to.

Be your own ultimate authority. Remember, growing up in a fundie home has made you an expert in theology, philosophy, and all related fields, even if your degree has more to do with Tom Sawyer than Thomas Aquinas. (Besides, all the world traveling you've done more than fills in the gaps.)

Master the art of the random simile. The Kingdom is like a pointillist painting. The canon of Scripture is like a green and orange striped bus carrying a marching band to an away game. The more bizarre (and unwarranted) the better (See also: sounding deep).

Debate

Theological debate requires you to amp up your usual tactics for answering critics (blog-trolling, see above). It's best to avoid theological debate by claiming the high ground. But, when you absolutely have to engage a live person, it helps to have a strategy. Follow these guidelines:

- Consider no one a valid critic. If you receive a letter co-signed by Billy Graham, R.C. Sproul, Pope Benedict, and St. Paul, calling you a rank heretic, just laugh it off. Maybe use it as an opener for one of your talks. Wear "heretic" as a badge of honor. People find that cute.

- Use guilt by association. Group your critics in with "Plato, Aristotle, and Caesar." Contrary to popular belief, this is a legitimate logical tactic.

- Come up with a catch-all accusation for your detractors. They're all Gnostic, six-line Greco-Roman imperialists. Or modernistic, close-minded, arrogant exclusivists. Or unsophisticated, fundamentalist thought police. Just make sure you limit yourself to using one main label. Once you've got it, throw that accusation out at least once per minute or twice per page. It needn't have any bearing on reality—if you repeat it enough, a certain sector of the population (the people who buy your books or read your blog) will begin to believe it.

Fig. 0

. . .

The best thing about debating Plato: he can't answer you. Because he's *dead*.

40

- It's important to bear in mind that the only reason your opponents don't immediately convert to Kinda Christianity is because they're scared. Acknowledge this and tell them it's okay. At the same time, belittle those who get their salary and social status from the "old way" of viewing the Bible. Do this well enough and it might gain you fame and fortune (like multiple book deals and your own speaking tour).

Scripture

If a narrative passage of Scripture doesn't serve your agenda when taken at face value, make up a fun back story for some of the characters or paraphrase their words in a folksy hipster dialect so that what they're saying is what you've been saying all along.

In our quest for Kinda Christianity, it's important to always be dividing Scripture against itself. Pit Paul against Jesus, Moses against Isaiah, even God (the mean one from the Bible) against God (the nice one who thinks exactly like you). This puts everyone off-balance, which is good for The Conversation (may it be forever praised).

Be careful when speaking of progressive revelation. You don't want to let Paul or John have the last word in the Bible, but you don't want anyone taking that blasted flood story seriously either. Just remember, *your* view of God is always the most "evolved."

41

Fig. P

You don't really believe that Moses came down a mountain with a list of rules from God. But if he had, they would be about reducing your carbon footprint.

Speaking of progressive revelation, remember: it's not as if Christ fulfilled the Law and the Prophets and should, therefore, be allowed to interpret them. Consult rabbis for that! The great thing about rabbis is that there are so many thousands of them to choose from, you will always be able to find one who says just what you were thinking.

Mock proof-texting as the context-violating work of simpletons. Proof-text.

Summarily dismiss the Old Testament. After all, it's just a bunch of made-up stories, starring a tribal, vengeful, violent God, who doesn't really exist. (Except when it makes a point you like, then quote it at length).

At the end of the day, the best thing about Kinda Christianity is that *you* are in control of the Bible because you get to decide which parts really count and what they really mean. You're no longer shackled by context, authorial intent, or reality! How freeing is *that*? Prophetic scenes that depict birds of prey picking the flesh from piles of corpses? Why, those are really about equal rights for undocumented immigrants. The story of Cain and Abel is actually a critique exposing the evils of private property. The elements melting like wax at the end of time? Eh, that's just St. Peter's way of pushing for vegetarianism, green energy, and socialized health care. Are you beginning to see the possibilities? It's like a never-ending Scriptural Mad Lib; luxuriate in it!

I want to get up and dance around my office as I write this!

Remember, there is no fall, there is no original sin, there is no substitutionary atonement, and there is no bodily second coming. Your opponents might conclude from this that you're a classical Protestant liberal. Which just proves they weren't paying attention when you said you're not.

CONCLUSION

So you've done it. You've moved through the birth canal that is Kinda Christianity. You've danced with us in the wild, unkempt, dirty, but infinitely satisfying dried-up riverbed that we call LIFE! Our guess is that you may never be the same. The coffee will taste better, the Guinness will be cheaper and always on draft, the theology will be less rigid, and the dance will look less-awkward!

Remember a few things as you go on your journey to Kinda Christianity: One, you will still be misunderstood. That's okay, embrace this! Remember that all of the great ones—like Pelagius, Johnny Cash, Che, and Bob Marley—were mis-understood. And if they weren't, they pretended to be because being misunderstood is good for business! Know that if you're joyful, content, and happy, then something is horribly wrong.

And finally, remember that the Revolution, the movement, starts with YOU!

Ted Kluck is the author of several books, on topics ranging from Mike Tyson to the Emergent Church. Both *Why We're Not Emergent* and *Why We Love the Church* (with Kevin DeYoung) won Christianity Today Book of the Year awards, and *Paper Tiger: One Athlete's Journey to the Underbelly of Pro Football* won a Michigan Notable Book award in 2008. His work has also appeared in ESPN the Magazine and Christianity Today.

Ted has played professional indoor football, coached high school football, trained as a professional wrestler, served as a missionary, and taught writing courses at the college level. He lives in Grand Ledge, MI with his wife Kristin and sons Tristan and Maxim. He once owned a used Volvo and has an impressive collection of ironic t-shirts. You can find his blog and homepage at http://www.tedkluck.com

Zach Bartels is a totally non-revolutionary, plodding, six-line Greco-Roman imperialist who gets his salary and social status from the *old* way of reading the Bible. He spends most of his time trying to worm his way into the pages of Ted Kluck books. (In this, he has been quite successful).

Zach lives in Lansing, Michigan with his wife Erin and son Calvin. He maintains a blog at http://twelve60.blogspot.com